WEDGWOOD
WARE

ALISON KELLY

WARD LOCK LIMITED   LONDON AND SYDNEY

Printed in Great Britain
by Cox & Wyman Limited for
Ward Lock Limited, 116 Baker Street,
London W1M 2BB

ACKNOWLEDGEMENTS

The author acknowledges her indebtedness to the researches of Mr. and Mrs. J. K. des Fontaines, Mr. Norman Stretton, Mrs. Charlotte Zeitlin and other members of the Wedgwood Society (England) and the Wedgwood International Seminar, and also to the State Hermitage Museum, Leningrad for information about the Catherine Service. She is also most grateful to those collectors and Museum Curators who have kindly allowed her to illustrate their pieces, and particularly to Messrs. Josiah Wedgwood and Sons Ltd. for their generosity in supplying photographs and information.

Photographs

Mr. and Mrs. Dwight M. Beeson, Birmingham, Alabama, pages 11, 19, 55, 58; Mr. and Mrs. Byron Born, New York, 72, 73; The British Museum, London, 31, 38, 52, 53, 56, 57, 66, 75; The Buten Museum of Wedgwood, Merion, Pa., 81, 85, 88, 90; Mrs. R. D. Chellis, Wellesley Hills, Mass., 18, 28, 56, 79; Mr. and Mrs. J. K. des Fontaines, London, 68, 69; Mrs. Hendrey, Essex, 39; the State Hermitage Museum, Leningrad, 36; Mr. A. T. Morley Hewitt and Mrs. D. E. M. Jarvis, London, 7, 36, 40, 42, 84; City of Liverpool Museums, 19, 47, 62, 63, 74; National Buildings Record, London, 86; Castle Museum and Art Gallery, Nottingham, 31, 47, 54; Mr. and Mrs. Norman Stretton, Oxfordshire, 10, 32, 33, 37, 42; Victoria and Albert Museum, London, 19, 80, 82, 83, 85, 87, 89; Messrs. Josiah Wedgwood and Sons Ltd., Front Cover, Frontispiece, 6, 7, 11, 30, 32, 33, 34, 35, 37, 38, 40, 41, 43, 44, 45, 46, 48, 49, 50, 51, 58, 60, 61, 62, 64, 65, 67, 70, 71, 75, 76, 77, 78, 79, 82, 91, 92, 93, 94; Mr. and Mrs. David Zeitlin, Merion, Pa., 28, 46.

Cover illustrations

Vase and Ewer in black basaltes, designed during the partnership of Wedgwood and Bentley, 1769–1780. The ewer is designed for wine, and has a satyr crouched with his arms round the spout, a goat mask on the front, and swage of grapes on the sides.
The vase has satyr masks at the base of the handles.
Wedgwood Museum, Barlaston. Late 18th century Jasper Plaque at the Castle Museum and Art Gallery Nottingham.

INTRODUCTION

Early Wares

Thomas Wedgwood established the Churchyard Works for the manufacture of pottery in Burslem in 1656, and it descended to his son and grandson, both called Thomas also. The latter of these Thomases was the father of Josiah Wedgwood, F.R.S., whose elder brother – Thomas again – inherited the works, and left it to *his* son, yet another Thomas. Other potting Wedgwoods were Dr. Thomas Wedgwood, who gained a high reputation, in the early eighteenth century, for salt-glazed stoneware, and Josiah's uncles John and Thomas who were the first Staffordshire potters to trade directly with London and Liverpool. However, though it can be seen that pottery was in his blood, and his direct ancestors had been making pottery for a century at a factory which he himself bought in 1780, it is Josiah Wedgwood, born in 1730, who is of particular importance to the student of ceramics; and the history of his firm is considered to begin in 1759, the year in which he set up on his own as an independent potter.

Josiah had a practical education in the trade, and might have remained a craftsman potter himself, if it had not been for an infection in his knee, due to smallpox at the age of twelve, which eventually led to the amputation of his leg. His inability to work the treadle of a potter's wheel turned his mind towards management, and long periods of enforced rest as a boy gave him time to think of new types of ware at that time unheard of in the Potteries. Such large ideas may well have influenced Josiah's elder brother, then managing the family firm, not to take him into partnership.

Forced to strike out on his own, Josiah Wedgwood joined a local businessman, John Harrison, for a short time, a partnership which suited neither of them, and then in 1754 became the partner of a well-known potter with a good business, Thomas Whicldon of Fenton Low. Whieldon's ware, as much admired today as it was in Wedgwood's own time, was noted for its marbled and mottled glazes, produced by dusting the surface before firing with metallic oxides, which melted and streaked in the kiln, producing random patterns.

5

Wedgwood, of course, helped in the production of this ware when he
was in partnership with Whieldon, and also for a short time after he
set up on his own, so that it is often very difficult to distinguish
between Whieldon and Wedgwood-Whieldon ware. During the
latter part of the partnership, Wedgwood began a series of ceramic

(Left.) *Vase with cover, made of* solid agate ware *produced by
'wedging', or kneading clays of two or three colours together, so
that the marbling goes right through the body. Black basaltes
plinth. Gilt putto on the lid. Marked* Wedgwood & Bentley. *c. 1776.*
(Right.) *Three-handled vase, stippled marbling on a creamware
body. c. 1775.* Wedgwood Museum, Barlaston.

*Detail of the mezzotint
taken from Sir Joshua
Reynolds' portrait of
Josiah Wedgwood, F.R.S.
Wedgwood Museum, Barlaston.*

experiments which, under the generous terms of his agreement with Whieldon, he was not obliged to communicate to his partner. The practice of making experiments, carefully controlled and recorded, became part of his life, and led to the characteristic bodies and colours associated with his wares. His experiment books and thousands of numbered samples of various bodies are now in the Wedgwood Museum at Barlaston in Staffordshire.

In 1759, Wedgwood was able to start in management on his own at the Ivy House works (leased from his cousins). Very soon – it is only no. 7 in his Experiment Book – he evolved a rich deep green glaze, of a colour not previously available for glazing the wares made in the Potteries. With it, he could imitate the 'cauliflowers,' 'pineapples' and 'cabbages' which fashionable people were buying in porcelain from the factories of Chelsea or Bow. Green-glazed ware could be fired in the same kiln as the Whieldon-type tortoiseshell and marbled wares with their streaky and mottled glazes, so that production of the standard wares could be continued while the new designs were tried out. Moulds were made so that the 'cauliflowers' or 'pineapples' could have their details modelled in three dimensions. Veins in the leaves were channelled, so that the glaze ran thickly into them and thinly on the convex surfaces, giving variations of tone.

In 1762, Wedgwood moved to the Brick House works, a 'pot-bank' owned by the Adams family (potters since the seventeenth century whose firm's independent existence was to end only in 1966 when it became part of the Wedgwood Group). The factory later went by the name of the Bell Works (from the bell which summoned the workmen) and here Wedgwood continued to manufacture his Useful Wares – table and dairy pieces – until 1773.

Queen's Ware

At the beginning of the 1760s, Wedgwood spent much time in trying to perfect an earthenware body of a cream-colour pale and clear enough to be glazed with a transparent lead glaze. By 1763 he had produced what he called 'a species of earthenware for the table, covered with a rich and brilliant glaze' which could be manufactured easily and cheaply. This ware was an immediate success with the public and was, in fact, the chief manufacture at the Wedgwood factory from the seventeen-sixties until the beginning of the nineteen-sixties. This earthenware was called Queen's Ware after Queen Charlotte, who admired it, and gave Wedgwood the appointment of Potter to the Queen. Early creamware can be distinguished from modern pieces by the thinness of the potting, which makes the ware surprisingly light to handle; an early plate often feels hardly heavier than a modern plastic one. The colour of early pieces is often a deep colour, like Devonshire cream, or yellowish. It gradually became lighter, and the body was much improved after 1775 by the addition of Cornish china-clay and china-stone. Soon after its introduction, every variety of domestic piece could be bought in Queen's Ware, so that a table could be laid with as lavish an assortment of tureens, sauce-boats, dishes, compotières, ladles, ice-pails and every size of plate, as could be found in the dinner-services of porcelain. Table-centres were also made; called épergnes, they are stands hung like a Christmas tree with a number of little bowls and baskets. Unfortunately they rarely survive with all their fragile cargo complete, but individual pieces from them can often be found. Queen's Ware could also be used for other domestic purposes. 'Night lamps to keep liquids warm all night,' shaving bowls and, later, bidets could all be supplied. By the 1780s, all the equipment for dairies was available, from tiling for the walls to settling pans for the cream. At least one dairy equipped in this way with Wedgwood ware has survived complete. Wedgwood issued an illustrated catalogue of creamware in 1774, and this is valuable in helping to identify pieces, particularly since creamware similar to Wedgwood's was manufactured at a number of other factories in the later eighteenth century. That made at the Leeds Pottery has great charm; a Leeds illustrated catalogue was first issued in 1783.

By the beginning of the 1770s, Wedgwood was sufficiently well known abroad for the Empress Catherine of Russia to order a large dinner-service of creamware. It was decorated with a husk design in mulberry-pink, has survived virtually complete, and is now displayed, as if for a banquet, at the palace of Petrodvorets, near Leningrad. This design was not made exclusively for the Empress; shards from a similar design have been dug up in Williamsburg, Virginia, from services broken by butter-fingered servants in the colonial period, and this pattern has been reissued in modern times under the name of 'Colonial Williamsburg.' The modern version is on a whiter body, and the decoration in a clearer pink, than the original eighteenth-century version.

In 1773, possibly with some persuasion from Lord Cathcart, the British Ambassador in St. Petersburg, who knew Wedgwood, the Empress Catherine ordered a much more elaborate dinner and dessert service, of no less than 952 pieces, each decorated with a different hand-painted view of English scenery. Though the service itself was not expensive, obtaining the prints and drawings from which to copy, and having the designs and borders painted on the ware to a suitably high standard, cost a great deal of money. Wedgwood's estimates show that he could have spent as much as £2,600 in producing the service, and as Catherine's archives record that she paid him just a little over £2,700, the financial profit for more than a year's work was extremely small. She did, however, pay immediately on receipt of the service, whereas many eighteenth-century tradesmen went bankrupt waiting for payment from dilatory monarchs; and the prestige value of the service was immense. It was put on show in London, and the Queen (whose gardens at Kew were illustrated extensively) and the nobility came to view and praise. From this time, Wedgwood's order books were full of the names of the aristocracy, so that a surviving ledger reads like a copy of Debrett.

The service was made for the palace of Chesmen, and was decorated with a frog emblem symbolizing the original name of the site in Finnish – Frog Marsh. It has survived almost complete, and is now kept in the Hermitage Museum, Leningrad (formerly another of Catherine's palaces) where a handsome display of it – even so, only about one-tenth of the whole service – can be seen today. A few trial pieces for the service are to be seen in English museums and private collections, and very occasionally one of the pieces listed as missing when the service was inventoried at the beginning of this century appears in the saleroom. Three of these have been sold in London during the last few years.

The Catherine service was a single spectacular commission; but creamware in similar shapes, but with only slight decoration, was made in huge quantities. Wedgwood paid great attention to what he called the elegance of form, and even the simplest pieces have con-

Creamware monteith. Transfer printed in black by Sadler and Green of Liverpool from a design in The Ladies Amusement *(1762) signed 'Pillement Invt'. c. 1770.* Norman Stretton Collection.

siderable grace. Many of them are closely related to the shapes of contemporary silverware. A tureen designed for the Duke of Northumberland by Robert Adam, for instance, can be almost exactly paralleled by a Wedgwood creamware tureen. The tradition of simplicity and fitness for purpose (Wedgwood always took home new tableware designs and got his wife to try them out, paying great attention to her practical criticisms) continued through the nineteenth century. A new creamware catalogue was issued in 1817, illustrated by William Blake, and many of the designs were continued for generations. Not surprisingly, this ware was disregarded by the late Victorian collectors who paid huge sums for Wedgwood jasper ware, and has only been extensively collected for the last 30 years or so. It can still be found, and it is worth studying the early catalogues, so that the characteristic shapes can be recognized.

At first, all the decoration on these pieces had to be painted by

Black basaltes ewer based on a classical Greek oenochoe, encaustic decoration. Early 1770s. Beeson Collection.

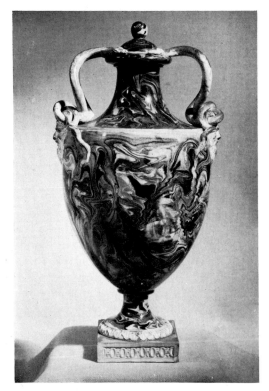

Early creamware vase of classical design. Marbled glaze, handles originally gilt. c. 1775. Wedgwood Museum, Barlaston.

hand, and the museum at the Wedgwood factory still displays the first pattern books, with delicate water-colour drawings showing border designs accurately in colour and scale. Hand-painted borders continued to be available throughout the eighteenth century, particularly for those containing family crests, but the rapid expansion of the demand for creamware outstripped the supply of capable decorators. A great deal of ware would have had to remain undecorated, had it not been that the firm of Sadler and Green, in Liverpool, had invented, by the mid-seventeen-fifties, a successful technique of transfer printing, by which a design printed from an engraving on to thin paper could be pressed on to a piece of ware and transferred to it. The designs were printed from copper plates, in one colour, and reproduce the linear effect of a copper-plate engraving. Correspondence between Wedgwood and Sadler and Green has survived; Wedgwood was scornful of Sadler's 'childish scrawling sprigs of flowers for the rims, all of which he thinks very clever, but they will not do for us'; and Sadler was urged to produce something more simple and elegant – 'Shells and weeds may be coloured as chaste as any subjects whatever.' With Sadler firmly under control, Wedgwood ware was sent to Liverpool to be decorated, some of it leaving from the port to cross the Atlantic. This arrangement continued for some considerable time, until the Wedgwood factory had its own printing section.

Some of Wedgwood's titled customers began to complain, after his creamware had been available for fifteen years or so, that they were getting tired of it. Tartly remarking that people would get tired of the archangel Gabriel if they saw too much of him, Wedgwood complied by making a body as white as he could and incorporating a trace of cobalt blue in the glaze. This counteracted the yellow and produced a nearly-white ware which he called Pearlware. Much less, however, was made of this ware. Something similar, under the name of New Pearlware was introduced early in the nineteenth century.

Wedgwood and Bentley

Throughout his career, Wedgwood wished to supply his customers not only with useful tableware, but also more decorative pieces. The earlier random marbling of the Whieldon type of decoration was developed into a more precise imitation of the fine marbles and porphyrys used by the ancients for the vases and urns which fashionable people brought back from their visits to classical sites on the

Grand Tour. *Granite*, *Pebble* and *Marbled* glazes, and glazing techniques, were evolved for use on creamware bodies, and Wedgwood
also developed an *Agate* body in which the marbled effect went right
through the piece. This effect was obtained by 'wedging' or kneading
different coloured clays together. Whieldon modelled some delicious
tabby cats using this technique, but it was difficult to achieve an
authentic marbled appearance. Many were the complaints from
Wedgwood that his workmen did not do their marbling artistically
enough. It was worth pursuing the idea, in spite of the difficulties,
since in this way he could sell pieces similar in design to those Greek
and Roman pieces collected by the cognoscenti.

Friends and customers such as Sir Roger Newdigate lent him
pieces from their collections, to use as models, and Wedgwood also
bought many of the illustrated books on classical antiquities which
were being issued at the time, and which graced the libraries of well-
informed gentlemen.

In this sophisticated use of classical source-material which would
already be familiar to his customers – so different from the practice of
his fellow Staffordshire potters, – Wedgwood was greatly helped by
Thomas Bentley, a Liverpool merchant whom he met in 1762, and
who became his partner in 1769. Bentley supplied the polish of a
classical education to complement Wedgwood's self-taught ingenuity
and enthusiasm; and the products of the period of their partnership,
from 1769 until Bentley's death in 1780, are by common consent
the finest in the history of the firm. Bentley went to live in London, to
handle the showrooms there, and supervise the painters who decorated some of the ware at Chelsea; Wedgwood remained most of the
time at the factory in Staffordshire, and a stream of letters on every
aspect of the business – new ideas, fashions, difficulties and triumphs
– flowed between them. Wedgwood's, which have been largely pre-
served, form a fascinating picture of eighteenth-century industry.
Bentley's have disappeared, but it is to be hoped that they may one
day be rediscovered in some neglected library or boxroom.

Wedgwood and Bentley celebrated their new partnership by a
move to a new factory. It was called Etruria, and the name com-
memorates the interest which both the partners had in making ware
which resembled the Greek vases which were being discovered in
Etruscan and Greek tombs in Italy, and which were always referred
to as being Etruscan. Sir William Hamilton, British Minister in
Naples (and brother-in-law of Lord Cathcart in St. Petersburg) made
the most important early collections of these vases, which are now

in the British Museum, and published splendid volumes illustrating them. Wedgwood had the books, and aimed to copy the pictures as accurately as possible, losing no opportunity of asking Sir William's advice.

To imitate these classical vases, which in the fifth and fourth centuries B.C. (the periods then most admired) had red figures against a black background, Wedgwood decided to use a black-bodied ware which would not need glazing, and to use on it some matt colours which, giving them a classical name, he referred to as 'encaustic.' He already had such a body available, since before joining Bentley he had successfully improved the traditional Staffordshire 'Egyptian black' into a densely black stoneware with a fine, almost silky, surface which takes on a slight patina in the course of time. This ware he christened basalt, or basaltes, probably having in mind the basaltic rocks of the Giant's Causeway which were a subject of much contemporary interest. On this black background, in shapes copied from Hamilton's books, Wedgwood's artists painted very creditable imitations of the Greek prototypes, using terracotta red, a brownish plum-colour, and white. It should be mentioned that Wedgwood in fact made his Etruscan vases in a way which is exactly the opposite to the original Greek technique. The ancient vases are made of a red clay, which is allowed to show for the figures, but which is completely covered with a black slip for the background. Wedgwood's much easier technique was to use a black body and paint the figures on it in red. As his red colour has dimmed a little, Wedgwood's Etruscan vases often, paradoxically, look much more ancient than their classical originals.

These vases had a great vogue. Wedgwood remarked that Mr. Cox, his London agent, was 'mad as a March hare for Etruscan vases,' and in one year the factory had orders for 350 classical ewers and 445 vases in one design alone.

The black basaltes ware lent itself not only to painted decoration, but also to pieces moulded in relief. Here, the inspiration was not so much classical, as classical interpreted by the Renaissance. Versions were made from works by Michelangelo, Sansovino and Fiammingo. There was a series of large oval or round plaques, intended to be used as wall decorations, and also a striking series of busts. The eighteenth-century library was not complete without busts of the poets, classical or modern, and from the early 1770s these could be had in Wedgwood basaltes as well as bronze or marble. The purchaser had a wide choice which included, as well as the obvious

Homer or Virgil, Milton or Shakespeare, the more unusual Agrip-
pina, Sappho, Rousseau, Addison or Chaucer. Neptunes and
sphinxes could also be bought for mantelpiece ornaments. Also,
surprisingly, the catalogue lists some elephants, 16 inches high, and
the pug-dog called Trump which belonged to the painter Hogarth;
neither of these animals, unfortunately, seems now to be known in
Wedgwood ware.

The black basaltes, dignified and sober, has never had as many
admirers as the more obviously pleasing blue and white, but has an
inimitable character. It is very effective for small portrait medallions,
and for intaglios – small plaques in which the design is recessed, like
a seal. Handsome vases were also made in basaltes. In George
Stubbs' portrait of the Wedgwood family, one of these black vases
has been brought out of the house, and stands on a small table beside
Josiah Wedgwood, as he sits at ease on a garden bench, contem-
plating his children. It must have had a special importance for him,
since it can be identified as one of the very early designs in the Shape
Book, still to be seen in the Wedgwood factory, in which he had all
his vases recorded for reference, as they went into production.
Wedgwood remarked that 'the black is Sterling, and will last for
ever'; it was in production throughout his lifetime, and at intervals
in the nineteenth century, and is still made today.

Jasper

The decorative schemes of Robert Adam, at the height of fashion
when Wedgwood was developing his business, turned the mode away
from the lacy rococo style, exemplified by Chippendale, towards a
more austere and delicate classicism. The Adam brothers were fond
of pale colours, blue, green or lilac, against which white classical
figures and scrolls stood out in low relief. Often the figures were set
in oval or round medallions, surrounded by thin tracery. To Josiah
Wedgwood (probably with much assistance from Thomas Bentley)
must go the credit for understanding that such a style could be
interpreted in ceramic terms, so that vases and ornaments in stoneware could complement the decorations in wood and plaster of the
fashionable Adam house. This realization led to the introduction of
the ware with which Wedgwood's name is particularly associated,
(and which many people think the only Wedgwood ware) the fine
stoneware which he christened jasper.

Experiments over a long period culminated in the commercial

15

production, in 1775, of a very fine-grained stoneware which was coloured throughout the body. It could be made in blues, green, black, lilac and occasionally grey and a pinkish mushroom colour. There was also a white, which was mainly used for modelling the details, but which could be used for whole pieces. Wedgwood had a strong distaste for shiny surfaces; he had to use glazes, of course, for tableware, but wherever he could he made use of varieties of stoneware such as jasper, basaltes, and what are called the dry bodies, caneware and rosso antico. Unlike earthenware, which is porous when unglazed, stonewares, being more vitrified, are non-absorbent and can be used for vases, bowls and so on. There are even black basaltes fonts. Wedgwood was therefore able to leave unglazed the slight patina of the basaltes and the almost velvety surface of the jasper. Centuries of dusting will produce a sober gleam on the black, and the apparently fragile bloom of the jasper will wash without trouble. These wares, which harmonize so perfectly with the matt and pale-toned Adam interior, stood out as being entirely different from the productions of his contemporaries. Only the Derby factory, which produced white 'biscuit' ware, and the Staffordshire firms of Turner and Adams, both of which turned out for a time very good variations on the jasper theme (in slightly different shades, and with different motifs), produced comparable pieces.

At first, jasper was used for small objects, medallions and what Wedgwood called cameos – imitations in jasper of those portraits of classical and Renaissance times which are made of semi-precious stones, such as agate, which are naturally laminated in two colours. The two-colour effect was easily imitated ceramically by making a base of coloured clay, and sticking on it small raised figures in white clay which had already been shaped in special moulds. Liquid clay, or slip, was used as an adhesive, and in firing the clays fused permanently together. Jasper, when very thin, is semi-transparent, and this can give a gauzy effect which adds greatly to the charm of draperies, etc. Wedgwood's craftsmen emphasized this by 'undercutting,' paring away much of the thickness of the white motif before firing. The amount and skill of this undercutting affected the original selling price, and is still an indication to be looked for today, in judging the quality of a piece.

Many of the early designs were portraits, either of well-known historical figures or contemporary eminences and people in the public eye. The fish-face of King George III, with Queen Charlotte whose early encouragement had helped Wedgwood in his career, could be had in a number of styles and sizes. Admiral Keppel became a national hero after his naval victory, and his jasper portraits were in such demand that Wedgwood had to write frantically to get the factory to turn them out fast enough. The foundation of Sydney was marked by the issue of the Sydney Cove medallion, which included some Australian clay brought back from the voyage; the storming of the Bastille (which thrilled both Wedgwood and his son, the second Josiah) resulted in three pieces, plaques showing the Bastille itself, with gesticulating figures on the battlements, and a more serene piece with a figure of France holding a long wand with a Cap of Liberty on its top. It was also possible for private customers to order family portraits, for a minimum of only six copies. Mr. Edgeworth, father of Maria the novelist, commemorated at least one of his four deceased wives in this way. Designs were also made from classical carvings well known to collectors of the day, such as the Farnese Hercules or the Duke of Marlborough's Cupid and Psyche. The Wedgwood catalogues, of which several were issued in the 1770s and 1780s, are a fascinating record of the tastes and interests of eighteenth-century connoisseurs.

Jasper was difficult to handle and to fire. There were particular problems in firing the darker blue pieces, since the colour sometimes bled into the white relief. 'The poor Queen's nose' was mentioned by Wedgwood as having been damaged in this way. For this reason, considerable use was made of jasper dip, a technique in which a white or pale coloured base was dipped into a slip (liquid clay) of a darker shade, before the white motif was put on. This very thin coat of dark colour did not bleed in the same way. Sometimes the edges of such pieces are polished on a lapidary wheel, revealing the original colour.

As time went on, larger and larger pieces were attempted. By 1777 or 1778, it was possible to fire large plaques up to 18 inches long and 7 or 8 inches deep, which were designed as the centre 'tablet' of the frieze of a chimneypiece. Large numbers of these were made, and it is a great pity that the majority of them were dragged out of their proper settings during the period of Wedgwood-collecting mania at the end of last century, so that they could be put in glass display cases. Fortunately, a number still remain attached to their chimneypieces in private houses. Mostly, the Wedgwood decoration consists of a central oblong or oval plaque, with smaller plaques at the outer ends of the chimneypiece; however, in 1786, Wedgwood mentioned in a letter that he was making six chimneypieces of a new type, in which the whole surface consisted of Wedgwood plaques, held in a marble surround. So far, seven of this type can be documented, so

17

production must have continued; three are in the Lady Lever Art Gallery at Port Sunlight, Cheshire, and another at the Henry Ford Museum, Dearborn, Michigan.

Wedgwood plaques were also used in furniture of the type designed by Sheraton, the most interesting piece probably being the piano designed by Sheraton and made for the Queen of Spain by Broadwoods. It is now at Old Deerfield, Mass. They also found a place in the decoration of candelabra and clocks, the Prince Regent's clockmaker, Vulliamy, using them frequently. Yet another use was for buttons. Lord Auckland, British Ambassador to France just before the French Revolution, once snipped a button from his new suit and sent it to Wedgwood, to show the fashionable Parisian size. A suit and waistcoat complete with a lavish array of blue and white Wedgwood buttons can be seen in the Bethnal Green Museum. Birmingham metal workers, such as Matthew Boulton of Soho, made charming gilt mounts for the medallions, so that they could be used for jewellery – pendants, earrings, brooches and the like. Chessmen were also made in jasper. Designed by John Flaxman, in 1784, they sold well until the end of the century; the Kings and Queens are said to have been modelled from the tragedians Kemble and Mrs. Siddons.

Large vases in jasper were not attempted until after the death of Bentley in 1780. They were particularly difficult to fire, and were sold for high prices. The 'Apotheosis of Homer' vase which has been at Audley End since the late eighteenth century cost 20 guineas, equivalent to over £250 in the money of today. Often, jasper vases were made in sets, to form a *garniture de cheminée*. Such vases were particularly admired by late nineteenth-century collectors, many of whom left their collections to museums, where this type of jasper is usually very well represented; indeed, to many people, the word 'Wedgwood' immediately conjures up a picture of a blue and white jasper vase.

Candlestick supported by three monopodia and Sphinx heads. An example of the Egyptian taste of the beginning of the nineteenth century. 1800–1810. Chellis Collection.

Man's suit – coat and waistcoat – late eighteenth century. Cinnamon silk with blue Wedgwood jasper buttons, gilt mounts. Bethnal Green Museum.

Masonic bowl used by the Freemasons of Etruria at their local lodge. Creamware with painting in terracotta and black, gilding and transfer-printing. This view shows the interior, with the transfer design of masonic emblems. Though the piece dates from the first years of the nineteenth century, the block for this transfer had been available for a long time, since its rococo decoration and the men's wide cuffs and large tricorne hats belong to the 1760s. The inscription is hand painted. City of Liverpool Museums.

Pair of plaques, light blue and white jasper with figures of Jupiter and Juno, in contemporary brass frames. These plaques are of large size – 7 7/16" × 5 1/2", and are impressed Wedgwood & Bentley. *c. 1778.* Beeson Collection.

While Wedgwood was still developing the possibilities of his jasper ware, he commissioned some designs from the sculptor Flaxman, then a very young man. Later, he became well known as the finest English sculptor of the neo-classical school, but he continued to work for Wedgwood from time to time, and to supervise the work of a number of younger designers working for the potter, such as Pacetti and Dalmazzoni, when he went to work in Rome. At the factory, William Hackwood, a self-taught artist, modelled for Wedgwood for many decades, adapting designs from drawings of classical sculptures; and designs were also commissioned from Lady Templetown, Lady Diana Beauclerk and Miss Crewe, ladies whose rather sentimental designs of girls and children appealed to customers for whom Flaxman's classicism was too austere.

Jasper is incomparably the best known of the Wedgwood stonewares, but he also made several other 'dry bodies' – unglazed stonewares coloured throughout the body – the most important of which are rosso antico (Wedgwood's elegant name for his version of the traditional Staffordshire redware) and caneware. Both can be found in characteristic Wedgwood shapes, but were also used in pieces following particular fashionable crazes. The colour of caneware, a soft buff-yellow, seems to have suggested its suitability for imitating bamboo, an exotic novelty which was painstakingly imitated in carved beechwood for chairs, or even, at the Brighton Pavilion, in cast-iron. Wedgwood's caneware can often be found shaped into a group of bamboo canes – four or six – cut off at different lengths and used as a composite flower-vase. Teapots were also made with imitation bamboo handles and knobs. Rosso antico was thought particularly suitable, at the time of Napoleon's expedition to the Nile, for pieces with an Egyptian flavour. Motifs from Ptolemaic cartouches are found on vases and pots, Egyptian canopic jars became the models for inkpots, and teapots had small crocodiles on the lids for knobs. There is even a set of Egyptian red and black dairy pans at Shugborough; nobody worried in 1800 that the unglazed surface was remarkably unhygienic.

The pieces which, for Josiah Wedgwood, F.R.S., symbolized the heights of his achievement, were his copies of the Barberini, or Portland, Vase. The original, of early first century cameo glass, had been discovered in the early sixteenth century and came into the possession of the Barberini family. An impecunious Barberini sold it in the eighteenth century, and it came into the hands of the Duchess of Portland (via Sir William Hamilton). The Duchess's son allowed Wedgwood to model from it, on payment of £100, a handsome hiring fee. The copies were made of black jasper, with white figures, and proved extremely difficult to model and fire. Problems of their production occupied much of Josiah Wedgwood's time during his last years of active work. Twenty-six orders were taken, but only about 14 perfect examples appear to be known, with about half a dozen having blemishes of one sort or another. John Wedgwood gave an early blue copy to the British Museum, where the original Portland Vase subsequently joined it. There is also an apparently unique slate blue-grey copy said to have belonged in the 1820s to Apsley Pellatt. It may be a trial piece, attempting to reproduce the blue-black of the original glass. There were several reissues of the design, including a Victorian one in which the nude figures were draped, and a monochrome version in which the figures, instead of being modelled separately, were moulded in one with the background. Since 1878, the Portland Vase has been used as a symbol in the back-stamp on Wedgwood bone china. In view of the number of reissues, of very varying quality, and the extremely high prices paid for early copies, collectors have to be wary in examining the examples they are offered.

The Early Nineteenth Century

The first Josiah Wedgwood died in 1795, a rich man, and the factory was taken over by his son, Josiah II, with the help of Josiah I's nephew Thomas Byerley, who had long been working in the firm. They must in fact have been running the business from about 1792, when the first Josiah virtually retired. The times of the Napoleonic wars were very difficult, and the fact that the factory did strikingly less well under their management was not wholly their fault. However, the drive and innovating enthusiasm of the first Josiah were missing, and we find the firm following the fashions rather than originating them.

Josiah Spode had introduced bone china (containing calcined ox bone) at the end of the eighteenth century, and the Wedgwood factory took it up in 1812, after Byerley had complained that cream-ware was becoming unsaleable. The first Josiah had not touched porcelain, which was well known for bankrupting a whole series of potters. (On one occasion he had been extremely vexed to find that a jasper stoneware experiment had produced porcelain by mistake.) Nor had he followed the usual practice of other eighteenth-century potters in decorating his pieces with motifs taken from Chinese porcelain, peonies, prunus blossom and mandarins. Early nineteenth-century Wedgwood bone china, therefore, with its Chinese-style decoration, was a complete break with the Wedgwood tradition. Chinoiserie, of course, had become extremely fashionable following the example of the Prince Regent at Brighton, so that the ware was very much in the mode. However, Josiah II did not much care for it, and startled a Swiss visitor in 1814, by telling him not to buy any Wedgwood china, as he would find better in Paris! To a modern eye, the ware has great charm, with its prancing dragons and bold flowers. There are also some delightful teasets painted with landscapes. Production of bone china continued until 1822, but in a trickle rather than a flow.

A similar style of Oriental decoration was also put, rather oddly, on a terracotta or black body. Previously, the dry bodies had been decorated with relief ornament in another colour, in the jasper manner. Apart from interior glazing, such pieces had a wholly matt surface. In the early nineteenth century a matt body was scattered over with flowers and other motifs painted in glaze, and therefore shiny. This odd combination of matt and shiny areas produced a ware with only limited table uses. It could not be used for plates, where food would have stuck on the unglazed parts, and is usually seen in such pieces as teapots, jugs and bowls, or for vases and flower-pots.

Transfer-printing, as we have seen, was well known from the 1750s, but for many years it was exclusively *overglaze* printing. The piece was glazed and fired, and the decoration was then put on the top of the glaze, necessitating a further firing. The fine lines of the engraved designs were easily damaged, and plates in particular are often seen with their patterns almost scratched off. *Underglaze* printing, with the pattern protected by a coat of glaze, was much more satisfactory, and John Turner of Lane End (who, as we have seen, made excellent Wedgwood-type jasper) is credited with having been the first to introduce underglaze blue printing in the 1780s. The patterns at first were of Chinese style, changing later, at the beginning of the nineteenth century, to elaborate landscape scenes. These pictures occupied the well of a plate or dish, and were surrounded by borders of flowers covering the whole of the rim. The whole piece therefore appeared in varying shades of blue, and the effect was entirely different from the expanse of plain creamware, with a very reticent border, characteristic of the early type of Wedgwood table service.

The Wedgwoods continued to have their ware printed overglaze, and were slow to take an interest in the underglaze blue which their fellow Staffordshire potters were successfully marketing. It was not until 1805 that Josiah II and his brother John (who had joined the firm for a few years) at last decided to order engravings for this purpose.

Between 1806 and 1810, eight patterns were introduced; some are similar in character to others being used at the time by other potters, but three are of special interest. The design called Peony has a rich flower pattern, four times repeated in the quadrants of the plate, which flows uninterruptedly from the centre right out to the rim. Another, called Botanical Flowers has on each piece a large single flower copied from a botanical publication. John Wedgwood was a founder member of the Royal Horticultural Society, and it was at this time that the Royal Copenhagen factory was producing its celebrated Flora Danica service ornamented with botanical drawings. The third is called Water-Lily, and an often-repeated tradition says that the design was made by Josiah I, to celebrate the publication of *The Botanical Garden* by his friend Erasmus Darwin in 1781. It would be pleasant to think that Josiah celebrated this hilariously bad poem by giving his friend the dinner-service, but though the family names are right, the generations and dates are wrong. The pattern is made up of a water lily and two lotus plants and again sweeps across the whole surface of the piece. The drawing of the plants is botanically correct, but this bold and convoluted design has a curiously Art Nouveau look, more characteristic of 1900 than its actual date of 1808. Until 1811, it was made in shades of rust, brown and gold, and the most extensive surviving set of it, probably the first issued, was owned by Dr. Robert Darwin, son of Erasmus, who married Susannah, daughter of Josiah I. The original, and very expensive, colour scheme was replaced by blue, which proved very popular. There was also a red version in the early nineteenth century. In Edwardian times it was reissued in a multi-coloured version.

In the 1820s and 1830s, several blue printed landscape patterns were produced, usually, like the designs of other potteries, surrounded by borders of fat roses and other flowers. One of these, called Ferrara, has been produced ever since. Unexpectedly, since Ferrara is inland, it shows a harbour with shipping; the name however has been retained.

The amount of Wedgwood blue printed ware, as compared to

23

that of other contemporary potters, seems to have been small, probably because the firm was in difficulties. The London showrooms – rather grand premises off St. James's Square – were closed down in 1828, and the old moulds and stock were sold. Many of the archives were also thrown out, but fortunately a large quantity of them were discovered, through a happy accident, and rescued by the Liverpool collector Joseph Mayer. Early Victorian and High Victorian taste, in which the emphasis was on richness of ornament, profusion of gilding and elaboration of shape, was in complete contrast to the austere elegance of the Wedgwood tradition. Minton was the archetypal porcelain of the time, and the pieces exhibited by Wedgwoods at the 1851 exhibition – eighteenth-century shapes halfheartedly given a little extra decoration – must have been outshone by the gaudy wares on all sides. By its first centenary the firm was in low water; only in utilitarian wares, such as the delightful pieces for kitchen and dairy, where the grace and functionalism of the eighteenth century were maintained, did the original spirit linger on.

There were technical innovations. A fine-grained stoneware with a waxy surface giving the effect of marble, and called Parian Ware, was used (in common with many other factories) for busts and ornaments. For Shakespeare's tercentenary, a new bust, designed by Wyon, replaced the eighteenth-century model. Lithography was first tried for transfer-printing, instead of copper-plate engraving, and there were even experiments in using photographic transfers, though with little artistic success.

The Later Nineteenth Century

The 1870s brought a change of taste. Eliza Meteyard's biography of Josiah Wedgwood had aroused interest both in the man and his ware. As the last decades of the nineteenth century passed, old Wedgwood was avidly collected, and huge prices were paid for early jasper and basaltes. (The creamware was thought hardly worth collecting, and much was used to destruction in nursery or servants' hall.) The old designs were reissued, sometimes in new colourings. Furniture inset with Wedgwood again became fashionable, some of it, by Wright and Mansfield, being of very fine quality. Lord Dysart ordered a whole houseful of fireplaces for Buckminster Park – the house was demolished in the 1950s and the fireplaces are now scattered in the United States. The firm exhibited an elephantine fireplace at one of the Paris exhibitions; it is now in the reserve collection in the Bethnal Green Museum. Bone china was made again from 1878, and has continued ever since; it is now the largest item of production.

In the nineteenth century, it was customary for an artist to design decoration which would be carried out by a craftsman. The first Josiah, with his moulded jasper decoration, was indeed already doing this the century before. It is surprising therefore that it was at the Wedgwood factory, and in the nineteenth century, that the artist Emile Lessore made a living by painting directly on to the ware; Stubbs had done this in the 1780s, but his paintings had been done to please himself. Lessore's work was part of the factory's output. Highly finished paintings, comparable to the easel paintings of the day, were put on vases at the Minton or Worcester factories, but Lessore's work is quite different. It has a lightness of touch which looks forward to the work of the French Impressionists. His work was mostly done on plaques or large dishes, each intended as a purely individual and ornamental piece, and is invariably signed E. Lessore. He worked for Wedgwoods from 1858 to 1875, at first in the factory, but later, on account of his health, at Fontainebleau, where the pieces he was to decorate had to be sent to him. Sometimes, and with very odd effect, Lessore's casual draughtsmanship is combined with jasper cameos and the precise shapes of neo-classicism.

Twentieth Century

The twentieth-century Wedgwood ware which has attracted the attention of collectors in recent years was mostly made in the twenties. William Burton, who worked at Wedgwoods at the beginning of the century, had researched into the techniques of lustre glazing, which had been introduced for a short time at the beginning of the nineteenth century and had then lapsed.

This early 'moonlight' lustre has a dappled effect, with usually a mauvish-pink cast showing through the iridescence. Probably the fragility of the lustre surface, which will not stand up to hard household wear, led to its being discontinued.

Burton evolved many richly coloured glazes, including deep blue and orange, and experimented with combinations of them with a lustre film, at the beginning of this century. His experiments were carried a stage further by Daisy Mackeig-Jones, who produced decorative pieces from 1914 onwards, in which deep colours, lustres and gilding were used in fantastic designs drawn from a mixture of folklore, chinoiserie and Art Nouveau. Her pieces, under the generic names of 'Fairyland Lustre' and 'Dragon Lustre,' in which the inspiration was mainly from folk tales or from Chinese K'ang Hsi porcelain respectively, were in production through the twenties and until her retirement in 1931, with some designs being continued until the 1939 war. A printed outline was painted in by hand; the piece was then glazed. Next the lustre was applied and fired, and finally the original outline design was overprinted in gold. The effect was very rich and, considering the diversity of her sources of inspiration, surprisingly homogeneous. She would have liked every piece to be an individual one, and in fact the streaking and flowing of the colours under the glaze did make each piece vary slightly.

Miss Mackeig-Jones used Chinese motifs in her designs, but her inspiration came from the highly decorated seventeenth- and eighteenth-century porcelain. A designer whose primary inspiration also came from China was Keith Murray, an architect who worked for Wedgwoods during the thirties. The Chinese wares which interested him, however, were the austere and elegant pieces made in the early years of the Christian era, and also early Korean pottery. The beautiful shapes of these early wares were, in Murray's work, combined with a high technical precision, probably inspired by his admiration for the Bauhaus. He made much use of engine-turned decoration, reviving a technique on which the original Josiah Wedgwood had greatly relied. Glazes for these pieces had a semi-matt or eggshell glaze, usually in cream colour (the favourite furnishing colour of the thirties was 'off-white') or the grey-greens of early Chinese celadon wares. The felicity of some of the shapes achieved by Murray should qualify them as the antiques of the future.

Wedgwood Marks

The Wedgwood factory was among the first to have a consistent policy of marking wares, not with a symbol such as the early Chelsea anchor, but with the name of the firm. Not all early pieces are marked, and it was as late as the end of 1772 that Wedgwood said 'we are going upon a plan to mark the whole if practicable.'

Creamware

Marked with the word Wedgwood or WEDGWOOD, impressed,

on early pieces. Often the stamp has been pressed in unevenly, so that the word may be half obliterated, and can only be distinguished from casual scratches by a careful examination. The word is not centred, and may appear at any point on the base. Some pieces are unmarked, and can be identified as Wedgwood only by a detailed comparison with known Wedgwood pieces and the early pattern-book illustrations. As a great deal of unmarked late eighteenth-century creamware of very fine quality was made at such factories as Leeds, attribution of these pieces is a matter for experts. Some other stamps, at a superficial glance looking like the word Wedgwood, do not in fact belong to the Wedgwood factory. WADGWOJD and WEDG-MOOD have been recorded, also WEDGEWOOD (like Wedgwood, a characteristic Staffordshire name).

Modern creamware normally has the name printed on it under-glaze. Since 1891, U.S. Tariff regulations have dictated the fact that the words *England* or *Made in England* should also appear. The current mark WEDGWOOD *of Etruria and Barlaston* has appeared since the move from Etruria to Barlaston in the 1940s.

The mark *Wedgwood and Co.,* or *Wedgwood and Co. Ltd.,* sometimes with a unicorn's head, indicates the product of a small and long-established firm which is not, however, Josiah's.

Jasper, Basaltes, Dry Bodies

The most sought-after pieces are those with the impressed mark WEDGWOOD & BENTLEY, or Wedgwood & Bentley, which indicate the product of the years 1769–1780. The names could be arranged in several ways, in a ring, or with one name above the other – Wedgwood
& Bentley

WEDGWOOD
& BENTLEY

The word *and* is always shown in its abbreviation &. Some very small pieces are marked W & B. A seal-shaped mark, with WEDGWOOD & BENTLEY ETRURIA in a ring, was used on basaltes, Etruscan, and granite or pebble vases. These last two types of vase are made of creamware, which since it was normally used for 'useful' wares, would not usually be expected to have a Wedgwood & Bentley mark. The partnership with Bentley was only for 'ornamental' wares; Wedgwood manufactured the 'useful' wares in partnership with his cousin Thomas, who had a 1/6 share of the profits. An ordinary creamware piece, even though made between 1769 and 1780, would therefore normally be marked Wedgwood only. The vases mentioned above were exceptions to this rule, as was the vast Catherine Service which, with its wealth of hand-painted decoration, was considered to belong to the 'ornamental' side of the partnership, and is marked Wedgwood & Bentley.

On the other hand, teapots and other tea equipment made in jasper, although obviously 'useful' pieces, were lifted, by virtue of

Ovoid vase and cover. Monopodia – animal legs with animal heads at the top – were used in classical furniture and copied for English furniture c. 1800. Here they have Sphinx heads in compliment to the taste of Egyptology. Gold lustre, 1800–1810. Chellis Collection.

Fairyland lustre vase and cover, 1920s, designed by Daisy Mackeig-Jones. The shape is based on a Chinese ginger jar; the decoration employs every kind of fantastic motif, in various colours underglaze, with mother of pearl lustre. Zeitlin Collection.

their decorative material, into the 'ornamental' class, and could have a Wedgwood & Bentley mark. (A number of such pieces were included in the 1781 sale held to realize Bentley's share of the partnership for his widow.)

Jasper vases were made, with a very few exceptions, after Bentley's death, and the mark, as for other pieces after 1780, is WEDGWOOD or sometimes (mostly in earlier examples) Wedgwood. WEDGWOOD became, and still remains, the normal mark.

Jasper and the other dry bodies are unglazed, and it is therefore possible both to engrave on them and to grind off markings. To engrave a Wedgwood & Bentley mark on a piece requires a high degree of skill, and is (we hope) very rarely attempted. It is however not very difficult to grind off the tell-tale word ENGLAND which indicates that the piece was made after 1891. A torch held level with the piece, at one side, will reveal the very slight hollow left by this grinding; the hollow is likely to be invisible by normal lighting. The intending purchaser should, of course, examine the quality of the jasper body, and the amount of 'undercutting' – hand finishing with a modelling tool – which will help to determine the actual rather than the ostensible date of manufacture.

Bone China

The early mark, from 1812 to 1822, was WEDGWOOD printed in red, gold or blue. When bone china production was restarted in 1878, a small drawing of the Portland Vase was included in the mark. MADE IN ENGLAND was added, as above, in 1891, and BONE CHINA in 1937.

Craftsmen's Marks

The original Josiah Wedgwood discouraged any indication of a particular craftsman's work. In the nineteenth century, however, it became customary for craftsmen to mark their pieces with an initial, and particular workers and periods can be recognized by the specialist. Three letter marks, to indicate date, were introduced in the 1860s, and continued to the end of the century. Their accurate interpretation is complicated, but they identify a piece as being made in the second half of the nineteenth century.

The artist Emile Lessore always signed each piece with his signature – E. Lessore. Keith Murray's pieces also have his signature.

*Whieldon-Wedgwood 1755–1760. The knife, marbled teapot and teapot
with raised decoration and crabstock handle were dug up on the
site of Whieldon's factory.* Wedgwood Museum, Barlaston.

*Pineapple and cauliflower coffee pots. Early samples of ware
exploiting the green glaze evolved by Josiah Wedgwood in 1759,
and imitating the ceramic fruit and vegetables made at the
porcelain factories in England and abroad. Early 1760s.* Castle
Museum and Art Gallery, Nottingham.

Red stoneware covered jug, engine-turned. This piece is unmarked but is attributed to Wedgwood on the evidence of the lid, excavated on the site of Wedgwood's Brick House Works. An imitation Chinese mark on the base incorporates a W. 1764–1769. British Museum.

(Left and below opposite.) *Tureen and teapot with flower knob. Such drawings were engraved to provide illustrations for the creamware catalogues of 1774 and 1817.* Wedgwood Museum, Barlaston.

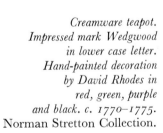

Creamware teapot. Impressed mark Wedgwood in lower case letter. Hand-painted decoration by David Rhodes in red, green, purple and black. c. 1770–1775. Norman Stretton Collection.

*Creamware teapot.
Probably decorated by
David Rhodes. The
reverse with typical
roses and floral
sprays. Dated 1772.*
orman Stretton Collection.

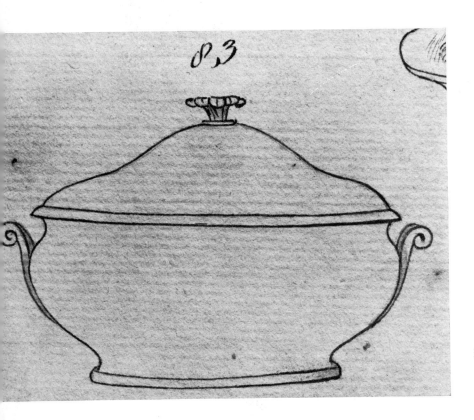

33

Three early cream-coloured earthenware vases. The body colour was originally hidden completely by speckled and marbled glazes imitating natural stones, and by gilding on the swags and festoons. This gilding has mostly worn off, showing the original colour underneath. The left-hand vase is marked Wedgwood and Bentley, and probably dates from the early years of the partnership, since it is No. 7 in the Shape Book begun at the beginning of the 1770s. The other two are marked Wedgwood. The centre one is engine-turned. The right-hand one is decorated with the 'Vitruvian' scroll design, and probably dates from the 1780s. The lid reverses to form a candle-holder. Wedgwood Museum, Barlaston.

Combined dinner and dessert service made for the Empress Catherine the Great in 1773–1774. It consisted of 952 pieces each showing a different English scene, hand-painted. This dish belongs to the dinner part of the service and shows Alnwick Castle.
State Hermitage Museum. Leningrad.

Two-handled lidded custard cups, leaf-shaped dish, in cream-coloured earthenware – Queen's Ware. The cups are illustrated in the 1774 Useful Ware catalogue, where they are shown on an epérgne. The border pattern is painted in greenish blue. The dish has a brown-painted edge, and brown spots on the twig handle, 1770–1790.
Hewitt-Jarvis Collection.

Creamware coffee pot. Impressed Wedgwood in lower case letters. Transfer printed in black by Sadler and Green with the Rural Lovers *copied from an engraving by Francis Vivares (1760) after a painting by Thomas Gainsborough. c. 1775.* Norman Stretton Collection.

Tableware in cream-coloured earthenware. (Left) tureen with lid on a fixed stand. Hand-painted armorial decoration in red and black. (Centre) *compotier with husk border and flower decoration in purple.* (Right) *compotier in the shape of a shell, with purple flowers and edge. The compotiers are of the early 1770s, the tureen a little later, though the shape is in the catalogue of 1774.* Wedgwood Museum, Barlaston.

Creamware transfer-printed plate, decorated by Sadler and Green in Liverpool. This firm decorated tiles; and a tile design The Hunted Beaver, *has here been adapted for tableware. 1760s.* British Museum.

Coffee pot and teapot, early Wedgwood Queen's ware, with printed decoration. Both pieces have spouts with an embossed leaf design. The slightly elongated globular shape is characteristic of early Wedgwood teapots. The Death of Wolfe *on the teapot was taken from an engraving made in 1776 from the painting by Benjamin West. The transfer-printing was done in Liverpool by Sadler and Green. Coffee pot c. 1775, teapot 1776–1780.* Wedgwood Museum, Barlaston.

Oval creamware dish and plate, feather edge, with printed motifs of scenery. Late eighteenth century. Hendrey Collection.

A page from the first pattern book for hand-painted borders on tableware, begun by Josiah Wedgwood F.R.S. c. 1770. The number patterns are painted accurately in watercolours on one page, and the identifying pattern names are written on the page opposite. The same design could often be had in two or more colour-schemes. This pattern book was kept up until the early nineteenth century. Wedgwood Museum, Barlaston.

Tableware, creamware shape of the 1770s and 1780s. all with hand-painted borders. In the background is a herring dish, with an embossed fish. The sugar box and cover (left) have the same border pattern in brown. In the foreground is a custard cup and cover, with an oak border in green and brown. On the right is a cream jug with a strawberry-leaf pattern in green, brown and gold. All the patterns come from the first pattern book begun in 1770. Wedgwood Museum, Barlaston.

Cress dish, cream-coloured earthenware – Queen's ware. The shape is No. 1046 in the 1817 Wedgwood catalogue. Painted border of pink ribbon with black dart motif. Base fretted and on four pointed feet. Late eighteenth century. Mosley Hewitt-Jarvis Collection.

Creamware plate with shell edge, hand painted in purple monochrome. Decorator's mark L in purple on back. (A Joseph Linley was employed at the Chelsea decorating establishment.) c. 1765–1770. Norman Stretton Collection.

*Creamware plate with hand-painted vine border, typical of the
designs in the first pattern book. About 1780.* Wedgwood Museum,
Barlaston.

*Cruet stand, cream-coloured earthenware – Queen's ware – made for
the French market, the lettering on the bottles being in black.
Such pieces were made from the 1770s onwards, and several designs
are illustrated in the 1774 and 1817 catalogues. This set could
have been made after the Commercial Treaty with France in 1786,
which increased trade with France until the Revolution.* Mosley
Hewitt-Jarvis Collection.

Creamware vases with engine-turning on the lids and bodies. Built-up flower-shaped knobs on the lids. Examples of the 'elegance of form' which Wedgwood aimed at from the first. c. 1780. Wedgwood Museum, Barlaston.

Creamware jugs. (Left) Liverpool-shape jug made for the Staffordshire Regiment in 1786. Hand-painted border and multi-coloured scene. Compare with the Ravilious jug on page 87. (Right) jug with a transfer-printed scene, and a hand-painted border in red and brown, with the initials J.F. under the spout. c. 1770. Wedgwood Museum, Barlaston.

Vase and cover, black basaltes with encaustic painting in red. The shape is classical and one side is painted with three Etruscan figures and an inscription Artes Etruriae ren-ascuntur *('The arts of Etruria are reborn'). This side shows that it was one of the six made in the first day's work at the new Etruria factory. Wedgwood threw them, and Bentley worked the potter's wheel. June 13th, 1769. Wedgwood Museum, Barlaston.*

Greek volute krater (left) *of the 4th century* B.C., *and its Wedgwood copy* (right). *The original was in Sir William Hamilton's collection (hence the H on the base, which has now been removed) and is now in the British Museum. It is 2 feet 10 7/8 inches high. The Wedgwood copy illustrated here is 3 feet high; there is a further copy 2 feet 9 inches high in the Victoria and Albert Museum, and it is believed that a third was made. These are the largest known early Wedgwood pieces, though there is documentation for even larger pieces not now traceable. c. 1780–1790.* Zeitlin Collection and British Museum.

Black basaltes vase with Etruscan decoration in 'encaustic' colours. Lion handles and widow figure on lid. The painted figures were copied from illustrations in Sir William Hamilton's books on his collection of classical vases. Early 1770s. Castle Museum and Art Gallery, Nottingham.

Seated Venus. Early basaltes figure from the collection of Joseph Mayer, one of the earliest and best-informed Wedgwood collectors of the mid-nineteenth century. Wedgwood bought a model of Ceres, a girl sitting in 1770, and she was on sale in 1774 in basaltes. She could have been turned into Venus by the addition of the billing doves shown here, which are emblemical of this goddess. Very large basaltes figures such as these are characteristic models of the early 1770s. City of Liverpool Museums.

*Basaltes plaques designed to be set in the walls of libraries,
halls, etc. The designs are from Renaissance bronzes by Guglielmo
della Porta, and these pieces show traces of bronzing, to make a
more exact imitation of the originals.* Left – the Feast of the
Gods; *right* – the War between Jupiter and the Titans. *11″ wide.
Wedgwood sent a specimen of the* Feast *to Bentley in 1771, remarking how difficult it was to make the integral frames satis-
factorily. These plaques, without the frames, were made from 1768.*
Wedgwood Museum, Barlaston.

Pair of ewers, in black basaltes. (Left) Sacred to Bacchus, *with a satyr clasping the neck, wreaths of vines, and a goat's head mask below the spout.* (Right) Sacred to Neptune, *with a triton clasping the neck, a dolphin's mask below the spout, and wreaths of seaweed. Both 16" high. Designed by John Flaxman, who was paid 3 guineas, in 1775.* Wedgwood Museum, Barlaston.

*Black basaltes teapot and cup and saucer. The teapot is very
similar, except that it has a straight spout and a lion instead of
a knob on the lid, to design No. 67 in the 1774 creamware catalogue. This pot is probably c. 1778. Engine-turning has been used
to ornament the body. The cup and saucer have decoration based on
Greek motif in encaustic colours.* Wedgwood Museum,
Barlaston.

*Young Marcus Aurelius, black basaltes bust 16½″ high. Modelled c.
1775, from a plaster cast of a classical bust bought from Hoskins
and Grant. A bust of the adult Marcus Aurelius was modelled at
about the same time. Wedgwood and Bentley.* Wedgwood Museum,
Barlaston.

Isaac Newton and Sir Joseph Banks, two exceptionally large blue and white jasper plaques, $11'' \times 8''$. The Newton is a technical feat, since the nose rises $2''$ above the background. Made c. 1778, and in contemporary gilt metal frames. Banks, the botanist, sailed to Australia with Captain Cook. British Museum.

Rhyton, or classical ewer or drinking vessel, in black basaltes, c. 1780. Copied very accurately by Wedgwood from a bronze original, c. 400 B.C., now in the Louvre.
British Museum.

John Flaxman and his wife. Examples of the jasper portrait medallions. Flaxman, later one of the most important English sculptors of the neo-classical school, modelled for Wedgwood from 1775 to c. 1790.
British Museum.

*Vase and cover with a portrait of George, Prince of Wales, later
Prince Regent and then George IV, surmounted by Prince of Wales
Feathers. Britannia presides on the cover, and the lion and the
unicorn sit on the base. The Prince came of age in 1783, and
this seems a probable date for the vase. The base is jasper of
a shade between stone-colour and pea-green, with a pale blue
jasper vase. The decoration and animals are white.* Castle Museum
and Art Gallery, Nottingham.

The eighteenth-century taste for ruins. Three ruined columns and ruined vase in blue and white jasper, to satisfy the taste for dilapidated archaeological fragments enjoyed by the Georgian connoisseur. Sir William Chambers, in similar mood, designed the Ruined Arch *in Kew Gardens. 1780s.* Beeson Collection.

*Jasper medallion in memor[y]
Salomon Gessner, 1730–17[..]
painter and engraver. Versi[on]
in miniature of the late eightee[nth]
century funerary monuments
with classical figures weepin[g]
over a portrait. c. 1790.
Chellis Collection.*

*Blue jasper plaque and vase, both with the same design
by John Flaxman* The Apotheosis of Homer, *based
on one of Hamilton's vases. The plaque was for the
central feature of a chimneypiece and was made by 1778.
The vase, with a model of Pegasus on top, dates from
1786, when Wedgwood presented it to the British Museum.*
British Museum.

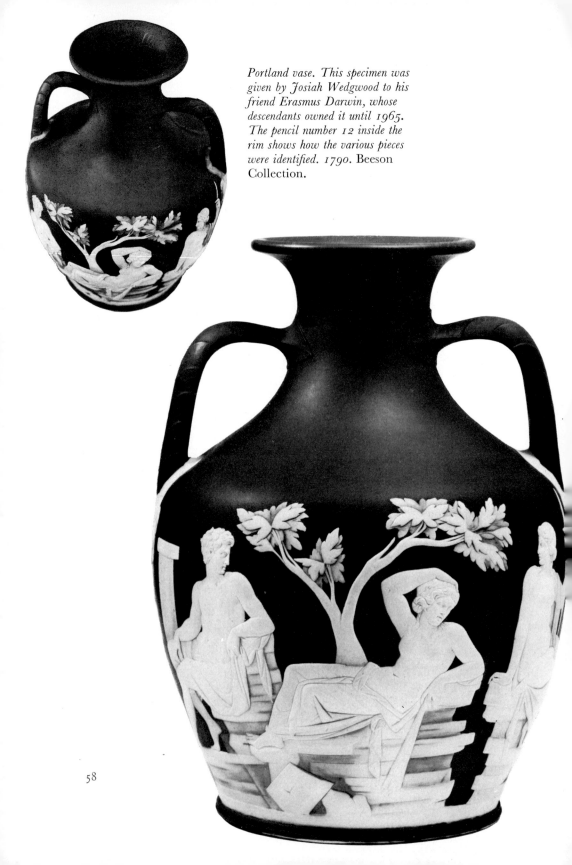

Portland vase. This specimen was given by Josiah Wedgwood to his friend Erasmus Darwin, whose descendants owned it until 1965. The pencil number 12 inside the rim shows how the various pieces were identified. 1790. Beeson Collection.

Jasper vases, two out of a set of three designed as a garniture de cheminée. *White on black. The larger one was put in the centre.* (Left) Sacrifice to Ceres, (Right) Venus in her chariot drawn by swans. *c. 1790.* Wedgwood Museum, Barlaston.

Portland Vase, black jasper with white jasper figures, late 1780s. A copy of an Alexandrian glass vase of c. 30 B.C. *to* A.D. *30., brought from Italy by Sir William Hamilton, and now in the British Museum.* Wedgwood Museum, Barlaston.

*Two teapots and a covered milk jug in jasper ware, late eighteenth and early
nineteenth centuries. The designs, by Lady Templetown, show – right-hand teapot
and jug – the design she called* Domestic Employment, *which was put into
production in the early 1780s. The left-hand teapot shows* Charlotte at
the tomb of Werther *from Goethe's* Sorrows of Werther, *an indication of
the impact of this book, published in 1774. The design of this teapot,
and of the milk jug, suggest dates in the 1780s. The teapot on the
right is later; its shape suggests the silverware designs of Paul
Storr, and a date of 1805–1810.*

Jasper scent bottles, from 2½" to about 4" long.
The designs include Zephyrs, *nymphs with gauzy wings,* Venus and Cupid
(top left), *a portrait* (top right), *a sacrifice*
scene and a Greek warrior, with a variety of
borders. The reverses of these bottles would have
appropriate companion designs. 1780s. All
Wedgwood Museum, Barlaston.

Scent bottle inset with a black and white jasper
cameo designed by Lady Templetown – Domestic
Employment. *Pin box inset with a blue and white*
cameo in the lid, set in cut steel. Inside is a
pincushion with hand-made eighteenth-century pins.
Opera glass, telescopic monocular with ivory eyepiece and blue
jasper drum with the Marriage of Cupid and Psyche.
All late 1780s.

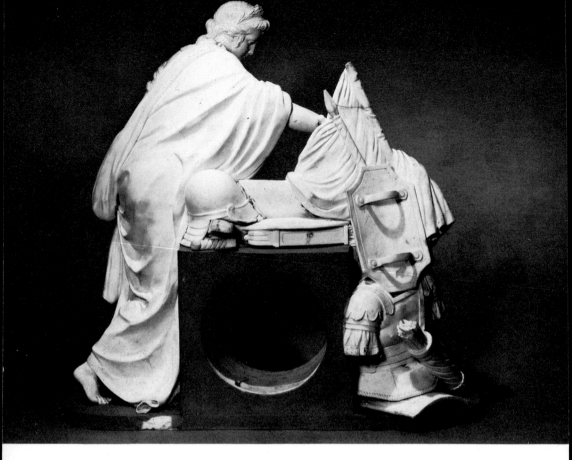

Back and front views of a jasper clock case; the clock fits in the circular opening. Designed to be placed so that the back view as well as the front could be seen. Figures of a similar type, made in Derby biscuit porcelain, appear on Vulliamy clocks. This appears to be the only Wedgwood example known. c. 1800. City of Liverpool Museums.

Chessmen, King and Queen in jasper, designed by John Flaxman in 1784. The actor John Philip Kemble is said to have been the model for the Kings, and the actress Mrs. Siddons for the Queens. Chessmen cost 5 guineas a set, when first introduced. Wedgwood Museum, Barlaston.

The dancing hours, a frieze of twelve dancing girls, arranged in two panels with six dancers each, designed by John Flaxman, and first mentioned by Wedgwood in April 1778. The inspiration comes from a marble and lapis-lazuli chimneypiece originally in the Palazzo Borghese, which was brought to England by Sir Lawrence Dundas in the 1760s. This design, in jasper, is probably the most popular Wedgwood decoration, and has been made continuously ever since the eighteenth century. Originally intended for a frieze for a chimneypiece, as here, it has been put to every sort of use, for vases, bowls, medallions and so on. Wedgwood Museum, Barlaston.

Pen and ink drawing by John Flaxman, showing the preliminary design for a jasper plaque of Achilles dragging the body of Hector, one of the series on the Trojan War. c. 1790. Wedgwood Museum, Barlaston.

*Bacchanalian triumph. A plaque of very large size – 21¼″ × 9½″ –
in a buff-coloured terracotta. This material was advertised by
Josiah Wedgwood as being an inexpensive medium to be painted over
in the colour of the room in which it was set. It could be for the
central feature of a chimneypiece, or inset in a wall, over a
mirror, etc. Incised on the back 1786; No. 70 in Wedgwood's 1787
catalogue.* Beeson Collection.

Caneware bulb pot.
As in the teaset
below, the yellow of
the caneware has suggested
a bamboo motif, here
carried through more
thoroughly. Painted
decoration in red,
blue and green. The
interior was filled with
soil and planted with
bulbs, which grew
through the holes in the
lid. The interior was
glazed. 1790–1800.
Wedgwood Museum,
Barlaston.

Clock, marble and bronze with a
blue and white jasper medallion
on the front. Made by the
clockmaker Vulliamy in 1799 –
one of a considerable
number of clocks displaying
jasper medallions made by him.
British Museum.

Caneware teaset,
consisting of tray,
teapot, sugar box and
cup and saucer. The
yellow colour of the
ware has suggested a
bamboo motif for the spout,
handles, and loops
on the lids. The
border, with a laurel-
leaf motif, is painted
in red and blue
encaustic colours. 1790–1800.
Wedgwood
Museum, Barlaston

Two versions of the water-lily pattern, designed in 1806 from illustrations in botanical magazines, of water lilies and lotus. The plate on the left is the version, in browns, printed underglaze, and gold, of which a large set was made for Dr. Robert Darwin, son-in-law of Josiah Wedgwood, and father of Charles Darwin. The plate on the right is printed in underglaze blue, with 'cut reed' border, and was produced in much larger quantities than the more expensive brown version. A multi-coloured version was produced in 1907, for decorative plaques. Des Fontaines Collection.

Plate, underglaze blue printed pattern, botanical flowers, introduced in 1810. The motifs were accurately drawn copies of illustrations in botanical books. The idea of these may have come from John Wedgwood, a founder member of the Royal Horticultural Society, and at that time assisting with the management of the firm. Des Fontaines Collection.

Plate, underglaze blue printed pattern, put into production in 1807. A well-designed pattern in which a motif is repeated in the four quadrants of the plate. A set of this design, with gilding and a Persian inscription, was made for the Shah c. 1810. Des Fontaines Collection.

*Early bone china teaset, a revival of the idea
of the Catherine Service, with hand-painted
individual English views. The teapot shows* Paddington
and Ullswater, *the plate* Brockenhurst, *the saucer*
Nottingham Castle, *the cream jug* Alder Valley
and Pinxton, *and sugar box* Brookhill *and* Saltram.
*The scenes are multi-coloured, and there are gold
line borders. 1815.* Wedgwood Museum, Barlaston.

Early bone china pieces. The teapot has a hand-painted landscape, the cup and saucer are the Chinese Tigers pattern, printed and enamelled, and the cup and saucer on the right are the design 'China embossed, gold edge' which is listed as No. 694. All were made between 1812 and 1822. Wedgwood Museum, Barlaston.

(Above) *This tableware has painted landscape scenes by John Cutts.*
(Opposite, top) *Cup, saucer and plate with puce-coloured decoration.*
Red Mark Wedgwood. (Centre) *Red Mark Wedgwood with bird motifs.*
The very rare bird designs are attributed to Aaron Steele. (Bottom)
Willow Pattern cup and plate and Chinese Tigers cup and plate,
painted and enamelled. Born Collection.

Candleholder of black
basaltes on tripod
stand composed of
classical monopodia.
These were adapted
from the legs of
classical chairs and
tables. Here, instead
of the usual lion's
head, there are
Egyptian sphinxes'
heads, to gratify the
taste for Egyptian
antiquities of the
beginning of the
nineteenth century.
c. 1805. City of
Liverpool Museums.

Teapot and stand, early nineteenth-century bone china with gilt
decoration. The shape appears to be No. 1467 in the 1817 Wedgwood
catalogue, and the piece must have been made between 1812 and 1822.
Wedgwood Museum, Barlaston.

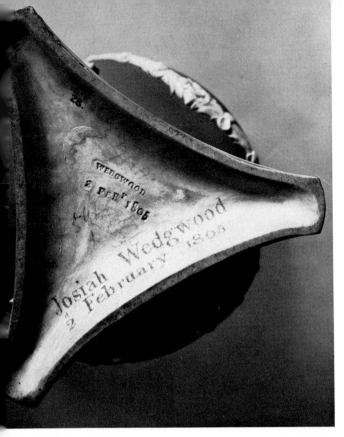

A Wedgwood puzzle. A series of tripod vases in basalt and jasper have the mark Josiah Wedgwood 2d February 1805. At this moment, the second Josiah was away from the firm which was being substantially managed by his brother John. The date appears commemorative, like the First Day's Vases (see page 46) but the occasion has not been identified. British Museum.

Two black basaltes mugs. (Left) *engine-turned with relief figure of*
a putto Bringing Home the Game. *Silver-mounted rim. c. 1785.*
(Right) *mug moulded in a beehive pattern. 1830.* Wedgwood Museum,
Barlaston.

Black basaltes crocus-pot.
The animal was filled with
soil and planted with crocuses,
which grew through the holes,
the foliage making the
'spines'. c. 1775. Wedgwood
Museum, Barlaston.

Early nineteenth-century teapot. Dry body, with applied decoration in white, 'crabstock' handle and spout, and handle on the lid also in the form of a twig. Parapet top. The glaze on the interior can be seen inside the spout. A similar teapot, though without the parapet, is illustrated in the 1817 Wedgwood catalogue, and is priced at 1/3d. Wedgwood Museum, Barlaston.

Plate, creamware decorated with Chinese Figures *pattern enamelled in colours in panels against an orange background. An example of the taste for Chinoiserie in the early nineteenth century. Date c. 1815.* Formerly in the collection of Sir George Barnes.

Wall pocket for flowers in the shape of a nautilus shell, creamware with splashed pink lustre glaze. Compare with the nautilus compotier shown on page 82. c. 1810. Wedgwood Museum, Barlaston.

Goblet, moonlight lustre with gilt rim. Beginning of nineteenth century. Chellis Collection.

*Octagonal dish with a transfer-printed design of oriental style.
Of Wedgwood Stone China.* Victoria and Albert Museum.

Plate of Wedgwood Stone China, produced between 1820 and 1861. It is denser than bone china, greyish and opaque. The pattern is printed and enamelled overglaze. This ware has a printed mark; Wedgwood's Stone China. Buten Museum of Wedgwood.

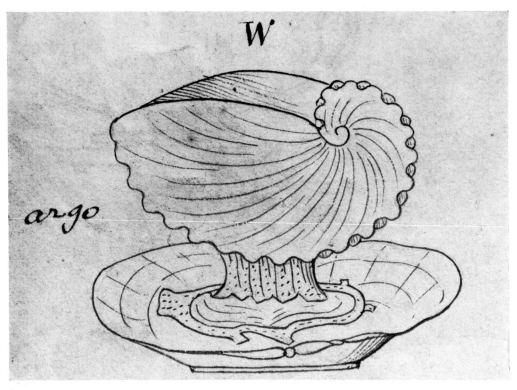

Design for a nautilus shell centrepiece for a dessert set. Josiah Wedgwood was fond of shells, which he considered a chaste form of decoration. Compare this drawing with the nautilus shell wall-pocket shown on page 79. Wedgwood Museum, Barlaston.

*Leaf, patterned plate, No. 434 in the First Pattern Book, 1805. Cream-
ware, with blue veins.* Victoria and Albert Museum.

*Tea and coffee pot, mid-nineteenth century. An early coffee percolator.
Tea was made in the pot (an early design revived; it is design No.
43 in the 1817 catalogue). For coffee, the pieces on the left were
assembled, with the coffee, in the top of the pot, and boiling
water was trickled through. Creamware.* Victoria and Albert Museum.

Vase of pearlware – white earthenware – with decoration painted by Emile Lessore, in shades of yellow and brown with a blue line on the handles. Signed and dated 1861. Lessore painted more usually on plaques and dishes; and vases are rare. The shape of this one is based on a Greek original. Morley Hewitt-Jarvis Collection.

Vase of classical Greek Kantharos shape, white jasper, with dark blue relief covered with a smear glaze which produces an eggshell finish. 1840s.
Buten Museum of Wedgwood

A mid-Victorian mixture. A creamware vase of classical shape (one of the early designs in the shape book) has been made more suitable to nineteenth-century taste by the insertion of a jasper cameo, and some scrolling linear decoration and a couple of putti drawn by Emile Lessore. 1858–1875. Victoria and Albert Museum.

Fireplace and panelling at Buckminster Park, designed by Halsey Ricardo in the 1880s. Green jasper plaques from eighteenth-century moulds on overmantel and cornice. The house has been demolished and the fireplace is now at 452 River Road, Narberth, Pa. National Buildings Record, Crown copyright.

Creamware jug, Liverpool shape. Decoration designed by Eric Ravilious in the 1930s. Transfer-printed in black, with trails of pink lustre. Victoria and Albert Museum.

Vase by Keith Murray, Queen's ware, engine-turned, and with a matt glaze. 1930s. Buten Museum of Wedgwood.

Two bowls, designed by Keith Murray in the 1930s. The larger one is creamware with a matt Moonstone *glaze. The smaller is creamware dipped in a celadon green slip, and engine-turned to show the cream body. The shapes are influenced by early Korean ware.* Victoria and Albert Museum.

*Coffee set, earthenware with a black 'Ravenstone' glaze, producing
an eggshell surface. Also made in the matt finish of black basalt.
Designer Robert Minkin.* Josiah Wedgwood and Sons Ltd.

Cream-coloured earthenware. The shape, EDME, was designed in 1908 and has remained in production, either undecorated or with designs such as this, based on the 1770 Pattern Book. Josiah Wedgwood and Sons Ltd.

Casserole, plate and teacup, oven-to-table ware, designed by Robert Minkin. Pale brown textured glaze with wreaths of fruit in natural colours. Josiah Wedgwood and Sons Ltd.

Grey-glaze earthenware, with a design in red based on nineteenth century engravings of clipper ships. Josiah Wedgwood and Sons Ltd.

INDEX

INDEX